MW01144013

by Rob Arego
illustrated by Adrienne Picchi

SCHOOL PUBLISHERS

Printed in Mexico

ISBN 10: 0-15-3584443-2
ISBN 13: 978-0-15-358443-5

Ordering Options
ISBN 10: 0-15-358357-6 (Grade K Above-Level Collection)
ISBN 13: 978-0-15-358357-5 (Grade K Above-Level Collection)
ISBN 10: 0-15-360682-7 (package of 5)
ISBN 13: 978-0-15-360682-3 (package of 5)

1 2 3 4 5 6 7 8 9 10 050 15 14 13 12 11 10 09 08 07 06

Here is a hen in a pen.

Here is a fox.
This fox can see the hen.

Can this fox get in the pen?

This fox can not fit.

This fox can not dig in.

This fox can not hop in.

This fox can not get in.
This hen can sit.